HOW TO BE RICH AND FREE NOW

Apply just 5 simple eternal money generating essentials

written by: **Sascha Të Light**

published by: **Freiheit. JETZT!**

May all beings be happy, rich and free.

Table of Contents

Welcome!

I am writing this book, because I believe that abundance and prosperity is the right to every being. Planet earth is a free will area, which means that all inhabitants are free to think, be and act as they like, as long as it respects the free will of others.

Everything we love to have and experience is available to us, we simply have to adjust our individual personal presence through the application of specific principles and actions into abundance, so life grants us as honorable reward with overflooding richness and prosperity.

What these basic principles, the 5 simple eternal money generating essentials are, you are going to know after you finished reading this book!

Enjoy!

Sincerely,

Sascha Të Light

How to be rich now.

Dear Reader, the upcoming three pages are going to transform your way of seeing so fundamentally, you are going to be surprised. Let the magic begin!

To start of, let us put things into perspective. Chances are high that because you are reading this book, you were either born or living in a western world country. Just this fact makes you so fortunate! You are already earning more than eighty-percent of the world's population!

Recently, I have been representing Microsoft at a new Game launch in Sydney, Australia. The job itself was not that fancy and the remuneration was really under-average for Australian standards. I was earning 27 Dollar per hour. The job was pretty easy, basically standing around and every now and then, talking to some kids. The other people in my team, who were with me there on that day, were saying things like: *"Oh, this is so boring. I have no idea how I am going to last throughout the day. I could really do better things."* I looked at them, happy and cheerful with a smile, which is always illuminating my face. I said: *"Allow me to say this. Do you know where you are standing right now? You are seeing the Harbour bridge and the opera of Sydney at the same time. You are being paid for basically just standing around. And just think about the world. Think about a young woman, born in Jakarta. Or Kuala Lumpur, Or Hanoi. Do you know how much they earn per hour? For doing what? To live under which conditions? Think about them, and keep them in mind, and then think about your situation again, how many people on earth would love to stand in your shoes right now."*

I know, I gathered this kind of view on the world probably because I was so fortunate to have been to so many countries before. I was not even mentioning, that how much money we earned in a day, is equally to the approximate average **yearly** income of an entire family in South Sudan.

So, really, when we think of our situation, we rarely put our situation into perspective. Knowing the world and being to so many places made me realize, grateful and really appreciative about the outstandingly fortunate situation I am in!

And this is simply a way of seeing things. The person I was standing there with, did not feel happy nor rich, yet I was standing there with her, smilingly happy and truly feeling rich! It is always a perspective and in every situation, through putting things into perspective, there are always reasons to see ourselves as fortunate and rich.

To be rich, now, is not about any amount on the bank account. Because, at which number would you start considering yourself rich? And is it assured, that you feel rich with this number? If there was such a magical number, every person, who earns, let us say 60.000 Dollar a year, should consider themselves as rich. Yet, they are not doing that. There are still people who think, that they are not rich, despite earning 80.000 Dollar! When we type 80.000 USDollar as our income in the calculator of http://www.globalrichlist.com, we find out that we are amongst the 0.10% of the highest earning people in the world!

No one in the world will ever come to you and say anything about you stating, thinking and feeling to be rich. You can be that, simply because you choose and decide to be so. And there are always reasons for that. It is our birthright as humans, because we have free will. We can choose to see the world as we like it to be. No one else can determine how we have to be seeing the world, it is completely an internal, individual decision.

The funny thing is, once you start seeing yourself as rich, fortunate and happy, life confirms that point of view. Life is not an objective thing, which is the same for you and for everyone else. It is different, life is not as it is, *life is as you see it is.* Life is the reflection of how you are and as you see the world. You see the things in the world based on where you put your attention and focus on.

"When you change the way to look at things, the things you look at change." Wayne Dyer said this. We always have the choice to see things as we like, to see the positive in everything and when we are doing so, life is so much more comfortable and convenient. Think positively and life is filled with positive thoughts and emotions and acts and experiences. *"Watch your thoughts, because your thoughts turn into your believes, turn into your habits, turn into your destiny."* - Siddhartha Gautama, the first Buddha.

Let me just exchange one word in a previous sentence.

Think rich and life is filled with rich thoughts and emotions and acts and experiences.

I welcome and invite you to see your life as rich now. You are rich now. And allow life to prove and confirm your view. Be patient. Be persistent. Persevere and you are rewarded.

Eternal Money generating essential 1: Live by a heart of gold

I started to be fascinated by this principle since the richest man of Babylon. In the book by George S. Clason it is recommended, to save ten percent of your income. In the German book "Reicher als die Geissens", the author Alexander Fischer shared his life experience of achieving prolific success. His wealth started to amass, when he started applying this principle. He called it **"The Money-Magnet"**. He set up a bank account, to which he transferred every month ten percent of what had streamed in. He explained it as an underlying energetic field of abundance, which is switched on, when this habit is practiced.

His wealth started to grow. Not just this bank account always grew, also all other bank accounts started to overflow with money. After one year he had become so wealthy that he stopped to practice this habit.

Within a short period of time, he had lost everything.

As he was evaluating his situation, what just had happened, he got the thought that he stopped saving ten percent of what he had earned. So he started again. Over the course of the following months and years, everything came back in balance, continued to grow and with him always and forever keeping on doing this activity, he reached the opulence of wealth he is enjoying today. He stated, that this activity is a major cornerstone of his success.

I started to do that too. I did it in addition not just in a bank account, I actually collected the money in one dollar coins physically. I kept track of my monthly earnings and they really grew from month to month. At some stage I had to drive to several different banks to ask for hundreds of one dollar coins to the surprise of the bank employee about this unconventional request.

I then had booked my second Vipassana ten day silent meditation retreat in Kaukapakapa, New Zealand. These courses were offered for free, while the organisation is relying on the donation of previous students to keep this offer free. At the end of the ten days, I had the chance to take a look into the books this institution was keeping in their library. I opened the book "The heart of Gold". It was a beautifully written and illustrated childrens book, where the prince was living in his wealth, always giving and supporting to the community. One day he was challenged by a fairy in his dreams, who was to take all his belongings away from him, to see how he would react. The next day, everything was gone.

Still, the prince kept his heart of gold and started to help harvest crops and grains to supply and sell it to the community. He still gave his surplus to people less fortunate with health. As the fairy was seeing that, she came shortly after, stating that this was a test and all of his previous, precious belongings re-appeared.

I somehow had this slight feeling already before I came to this retreat. I was just thinking of how much I was going to donate. Especially after reading this book I knew, I am to give it all. The assistant at the institution was quite surprised and had to count with several others for a long time to find out about the exact sum of the one dollar coins.

To be honest, I never felt as free as in this moment.

I learnt about Generosity already before. I met a beautiful woman in Cooper Pedy, who was doing financially very well, despite her youth. She credited all of her success to one idea out of this one book she had read. The book is called "The diamond cutter", written by Geshe Michael Roach, who had spent twenty-five years in a buddhist monastery to learn about buddhist principles to finally graduate as Geshe. During his graduation, the abbot, chief of the monastery, said to him: *"And now you are going to America and apply all the principles to the business world."*

He did and got into the diamond business. He learnt through being employed with one diamond-company, then founded his own diamond-company, which he turned into a huge success. The main principle and cornerstone of his ethics and culture, was to be generous. All wealth is created through the intention of Generosity, which is the sending of good will to another person, with the deep knowing, that there is always more than enough. When there is a situation, in which he, and also the woman from Cooper Pedy, was thinking: *"Shall pay less or shall I pay more, always choose to pay more."* Both always choose being generous and to give more. Which does not just apply to giving money, also in the sharing of knowledge. When she thought of sharing or not sharing what she felt as valuable information, she always shared generously.

Since my day in Kaukapakapa I switched from *saving* ten percent of my income to *giving* ten percent of my income. To be honest, the reward has not been an immediate pay off, as it commonly is. I was not giving that much and immediately received miraculously a check about a multiplied sum. Yet, I received the feeling, calmness and peaceful knowingness, that there is always enough for everything life intends me to do. It simply shows up in the right moment in the right amount. I am always taken care of and very well looked after. Deep inside I gained this knowingness that I am about to receive so much, while it was not the time for this yet, I just have to patiently enjoy my current circumstances now. And the day of abundant cash is going to come, for sure.

Additionally I have to mention, having this calculated budget of donation allowed me to contribute to some amazing organisations. I always felt so lifted when I donated and I knew and deeply felt that this is a true good activity.

Many people say that when they are millionaire, they will donate. As honorable as this might be, I believe, that we can become millionaire, simply through donating. It is not that we give - *when* we have millions - it is to give a percentage of what we are already having now. How shall life know if we keep the promise to give, when we will be granted a lot?

I believe life knows, through our heart of gold, of giving already now, in every financial circumstance.

Whom to donate to?
This is the happy time. You get to choose and find the sources in the world which you believe are doing sensationally good! This creates amazing good karmic energies for you when you are supporting and contributing to what is right and has to be done for the advancement of humanity and life on earth.

Fast-Track:
You are very welcome to donate and save/invest 10% each, which I found to be the extraordinary 'Fast-Track" to achieve your financial freedom. I am doing so with everything I earn and I can provenly say: it really is a true principle in life.

Eternal Money generating essential 2:

Spend laser focused

After these first words of a more spiritual character, let me share with you something very practical.

In order to grow your bank account you only have to apply this one golden rule:
Spend less than you earn.

That is it. That is the only thing that matters in order to grow and grow and grow and grow your belongings. I think this is so obvious, I do not have to further elaborate on this. Simply keep it in mind as the one fundamental golden rule.

What I do like to further elaborate on, is how you spend money. Robert Kyosaki wrote the book "Rich Dad, Poor Dad". Often times books are about a few key ideas and messages and the one of Robert Kiyosaki is about the difference between assets and liabilities. Understanding this is actually very easy:

Liabilities are things you buy, which only cost money and cost even more money along your usage. This is for example the streaming service "Spotify". You sign up with this service, and the only thing you get from it is listening to music. And you have to regularly pay in order to do that. To be very clear with you, this is not a very smart investment. This is just throwing out money, with getting nothing in return basically.

You like to get assets. Which means, you get money back when you spent it or they increase in value. These can be shares, as we will talk about in detail in chapter four. This can be special gear, which you use to do and create a special service, such as film making gear to produce youtube videos. See, you are spending money for things, which allow you to do something, which eventually lets money flow back.

As a rule, you like to absolutely minimise your spendings on liabilities in order to buy as many assets as possible, while always spending less than you earn.

A few practical thoughts on this:

- In line with Arnold Schwarzenegger in his early years, I do not like to spend a lot of money on clothing. Of course it is quite intelligent marketing that there are some companies tricking people to believe to buy a shirt, which they could get for 10 Dollar, ending up buying for 100 Dollar, because their special logo is stamped on it. As fancy and cool it might seems, actions like this are not prospering you quickly.

Still, attire is important. There is this saying "You are what you wear", which is very true. Statistics show that people are far more likely to buy something from another person, just because of the fact that this person is wearing a suit, compared to wearing a T-shirt. Therefore you have to have situational awareness, to wear high class attire in the right moments, preferably most of the time, which you can still get very cheaply from Op-shops/second hand stores. You can find amazing looking suits or costumes for a bargain and I recommend to obey of doing so.

- One of the biggest expenses is housing. I know that this is such a common expense, which many people have been trained to think that there is absolutely no way around it. Let me share this with you: In the past twenty-seven months before writing this book, I have paid for twenty nights maximum. How did I do that?

I am a trusted housesitter. Which means, I care for the pets of house-owners while they are on holiday. It is an absolute win-win-situation for both parties. Just thinking of what a person or family has to do in order to live in a house, sometimes with pool and spa? All the mortgages, interest rates, hours and hours in a job to earn the money to afford that way of living. And here I come, young and free, and ready to enjoy these pleasant homes. Of course I have to be a very reliable, trustworthy, caring, compassionate, well communicating and tidy person, which I am.

I know this is a completely different way of living to the standard, mainstream way of living, yet, it is possible! And I can honestly say, it is amazing!!!

– The next big expense, which we "have to spend" a portion of our money at, is our food. My recommendation is this: Eat less of high quality foods. The optimal way I found for me so far, is a raw vegan diet. I eat only highly nutritious alive ingredients in a preferably short period of time during the day. I was surprised how easy the transition went. Before I thought, I have to eat a lot, being a passionate bodybuilder. I love going to the gym and all advertisements and educators on the subject recommend eating 3000, 4000 or more calories a day. Which is a lot! Until I found this one bodybuilder, who eats just 1200 to 1500 calories in one meal a day and looks extraordinary! His name is Dr. Nun S Amen Ra. The decreased caloric intake is balanced out through the higher production of Human Growth Hormones (HGH), which are increasingly released in longer periods of fasting. I was able to cut down my solid food intake by almost two thirds and surprisingly, continued to grow even stronger than before in the gym! This cut also meant going from 400 Dollar a month for food down to 150 to 200 Dollar. Sweet as!

I also have a lot more time in the day that way. As we both know, time is the most valuable thing in the world!

I do have to mention, that this would not be possible with eating white bread, any kind of marmelade or Donuts, which could be cheap too, just not high in nutritional value. When eating less, the things to eat have to be as nutritious as possible! Which is given in a raw vegan diet, which I probably have to describe in another publication.

- Do not buy any stuff! The less things you own, the less you are owned. Buy the least things necessary and you are free!

- No alcohol, no smoking, no ice cream – why paying for something which is not good at all and does not contribute to health, longevity and a clear mind? Just enjoy life sober! It is the best.

- Also never buy a new car obviously, because the decrease of value is just extreme. Be very smart about everything you buy and keep the thought-process in mind: What is the retun on this investment? Is it just there, because it is, or is it actually rewarding me in the future?

Now, that I have been writing on things to spend less on, I also like to mention a few things, which I think are valuable and rewarding investments:

- Education, may it be seminars, personal development retreats, experiences. *"The more you know, the easier life gets."*

- Things that genuinely make you happy. Invest in the area where you know that this gives you a tremendous sense of fulfillment and happiness. May it be for your passion, your family, loved ones, friends. And always remember, be generous!

- Save/Invest and Donate 10% (Chapter 1)

- Jewellery and Gemstones (Chapter 5)

- Business and productivity enhancements, which are services or things that allow you to improve your creative output with an ideally higher reward. (Chapter 3)

- Assets (Chapter 4)

As you can see, dear Reader, life can be so cheap! It is about reducing all expenses to an effective minimum and spending laser focused on the things that matter the most!

Eternal Money generating essential 3:

Do passive income generating activities

We are free to do whatever we like, as an occupation. As romantic as it might be to be a veterinarian, the income with this occupation is obliged to time for money, time for money, time for money. Only when the person is there and is doing its service, the person gets paid. This applies to most jobs available in the world. Most people only get paid, when they are personally present. Which is okay. This can be fine, although already very young, I started to look into other options available. I found passive income strategies, which mean to receive money, even when one is not personally, immediately, directly present. And there is actually an abundance of possibilities! With my favourite one:

Books! Yes, what you are reading right now, is my passive income generating activity. This is the case, because something I have invested my time in to produce, is then available to consume for everyone, all the time. I can be laying at the beach on the Bahamas, enchanting some beautiful lady's and this book is bought all over the world!

Of course, to write a book which is an amazing experience to read for you, the reader, requires quite something. I have actually been writing many books. One of my first books turned luckily into a massive success, which made me persevere, even though my later ones were not being read as much, yet. It is like this with every skill, you do it and do it and do it and do it and the success is guaranteed. Because the longer you do something, the better you get, the more experience you have, the more rare and therefore valuable you are in the specific niche and skill you are in. Of course, there are some writers and self-published authors who have written one book. There are fewer with ten books and there are even fewer with one hundred books. Who probably knows more about the business of publishing books?

I also like to be really focused on being brilliant and exceptional in a skill, which combines so many amazing benefits like writing and publishing books. Books can be written and published for free. Books can be bought by billions of people. I can therefore inspire billions of people, how many can the veterinarian?

In case you are not so much into the writing and publishing, there are many other things you can do:

- Create and offer online video courses
- Produce YouTube videos (to some extend)
- Design and offer shirts
- Create and offer music tracks
- Develop an app
- join a multi-level-marketing company
- .....

There is really so much! Just research and find out, what suits you and your skills the best. It might start out as a hobby, something you do on the side to learn, to get better and might not be monetarily rewarding from day one. Persevere! Perseverance and patience is the real key to success. You probably have to practice it for maaany hours, or you are an incredible genius and do the exact right thing straight away! Everything is possible.

Just saying, if it was super super easy, probably everyone would be doing it. And since not everyone is doing it, it probably requires some effort to it. You can skip long years of self-driven exploration by buying educational courses from people, who already have achieved, what you are aspiring to do. Always learn more, learning always continues and with everything you learn, life gets easier and easier and also more rewarding. No bestselling author has been born that way, everything has been learnt and applied. So can you.

I also recommend to do something, which allows you to earn money online, because you can do it from everywhere in the world. When you reached a certain amount of income streaming in from it, you can just go and do it everywhere in the world! I believe that living in different cultures all around the world is one of the most personal-developing and maturing activity to do.

One thought to be remembered here is this one, which I recently learnt. It goes back to Adam Smith and the "Wealth of Nations". This eminent mister revolutionized the way industries operate with secluding the entire production stream in smaller sub-processes to increase productivity and therefore the output of the production. He came to this conclusion, because of this fact:

All wealth is based on productivity.

The higher the creative output of an organisation, may it be one person or a global company, the higher the revenue. Do more of what you do, because the better you get and the more rewarded you are!

Eternal Money generating essential 4:

Genius investing like Albert E.

With all the money you are saving now with your laser focused spending plus the increased flow of reward streaming in passively, you can do something fun. As already mentioned in chapter 2 with the core idea of Robert Kiyosaki, you like to accumulate assets. Assets are, in other words, income generating vehicles. This is the amazing fact, that you can put your money somewhere and just for putting it there, you are rewarded. The bank account is not a great idea to store a large portion of your wealth. Sure, you have to keep a buffer for living and some things that might come up, still you like to put some money away to multiply itself.

By looking into the different options available, the stock market is a very attractive one. The stock market goes like this:

Companies offer small parts of the ownership of their organisation. They are doing that to collect money. These small parts are exchanged and people can buy them, if they think, that these parts are going to increase in their value. In order to do this, one has to open a depot. Some regular banks are offering a depot, which usually come with higher fees. A short internet research on "cheapest online depot in my country" will give good advice on the best depot to operate with.

How to buy stocks with the best appreciation is the questions generations have been pondering about. I am going to share with you now what I believe is the perfect strategy.

Usually when you buy a share of a company, you can only buy it and get your money back when you sell it, preferably with an increase in value. Patience is the key word here as well, as the up and down and the different feelings connected to it lead people regularly to sell their shares when the sentiment is low. That is why quite a high percentage of traders loose on the stock market. Especially "nice" is this move, when the share, just sold, magically swings up again, because the sentiment has changed. I like to be clear, there is the chance of doing well and forecasting huge value-appreciations, although I find them personally not very easy to predict, in the short term. Based on these up and downs on the stock market, which is just simply the nature of it, I made the decision, that every share I buy, I am going to keep for ever. For ever and ever and ever and ever and ever.

I came to this attitude, because I coincidentally walked into a "Superannuation office", where accountants assist the management of the large retirement-depots, which very wealthy old man amassed throughout their life. I really was there by accident, yet on a very important purpose. One accountant was so friendly to give me a short introduction about what they are doing. Due to my curiosity, I asked very fortunate questions: *"So, what do the people actually recommend in order to amass large sums?"* The accountant answered: *"All of them actually follow the same strategy. They recommend to buy blue-chip shares and never sell them."*

"A-haa." Thank you very much for this amazing message, dear accountant. Blue-chip companies are the biggest organisations on the market. With them you have the certainty, that they will be around for a very long time, being suitable for retirement investments. I gladly kept this information in mind.

Yet I still thought that there might be something better to it. I remembered probably the most valuable presentation out of all during my studies at university. This presentation was being held by a person, who never went to university, nor was his lecture even connected to the university. It was organised by the "student stock exchange association", which is a small group of students, interested in the stock market and hosting events to inform about it. They invited one presenter, who shared his strategy on investing. He invested in dividend paying companies. He threw in some statistics, such as that two thirds of the appreciation of value in the stock market are in fact due to dividends.

Have you ever thought about this quote by Albert Einstein and how to actually apply it?

"Compound interest is the 8th wonder of the world. He who understands it, earns it; he who does not, pays it."

Compound interest is that you get interest on your interest. In year one, you receive interest for your base amount. In the second year, you do not only receive the same amount as in year one, you also receive interest on the base amount plus their interest from year one. As years progress, this compounding effect becomes vast. Just take a look at:

http://www.moneychimp.com/calculato r/compound_interest_calculator.html

and have a play around. For example, you have a base amount of 10.000 Dollar now and you keep it for 40 years with a dividend/interest paid once a year of 6%. After these 40 years, you already have 102.857.18 Dollar. After 80 years, you turned millionaire.

Now the question is, how to employ this effect?

There are actually companies, who have been paying dividends for 25 years and more consecutive years in a row. These companies are called "Dividend Aristocrates". You can again google this and get a sense for companies like this. The great thing about it, is that you can choose to either reinvest the dividend these companies are paying to get the great compounding effect or you can have them paid out. This way, your investment in the share of a company is not just a *"buying and holding and you only get something back when you sell it"*, it also is a passive income stream. Some companies pay yearly, quarterly or even monthly dividends. There are companies, which pay a 6% yearly dividend in quartely portions, so with a financial nest egg of 100.000 Dollar, you get every quarter 1.500 Dollar. In some countries you can easily live for 500 Dollar a month.

This dividend is paid, and on top there is the appreciation of the value of the company over time as well. On average, over the course of 10, 20, 50 years, the value of the stock market has been and is growing by an average 8 to 12% per year. Of course, some years it goes a bit down, still, most years the value appreciates.

This strategy is not a very "sexy" strategy and overlooked by many. It is the sure, patient and guaranteed way to wealth, not the quick way. Most people like to be millionaire tomorrow and do not become it, because the strategies are not reliable. This one is, and guarantees it in a couple of years.

Dear Reader, my recommendation is to build up a portfolio of different dividend paying assets with the thought in mind to never ever sell them. Especially in the early years, I recommend to re-invest the dividend. The more money you put in as early as possible, the sooner your dividend payout becomes actually an amount, which you can comfortably live on. And yes, you can speed up the process through using loans. By the time you retire, in 30 to 50 years, it definitely turned into a huge amount. This strategy is the guaranteed and convenient way to amass large sums of wealth.

The quick way, with large returns quickly, is to master chapter 3 and become supremely good at what you do. The better you are, the fewer are as good as you, and as we know from jewellery and gemstones, the rarer something is, the higher the value. And this is what we are going to dive into in chapter 5 now.

Eternal Money generating essential 5:

"Do we make our fortunes or do our fortunes make us?"

Depending on how well you know me, dear Reader, I am also a professional actor. I have been acting in the BBC-Production "The Luminaries", which is based on an award-winning novel, written by New Zealand-writer Eleanor Catton. I was in the room when Eva Green, famous for being the Bond-girl at Casino Royale, said the pretty spectacular line, which is one reason of the fame of the book:

"Do we make our fortunes, or do our fortunes make us?"

I invite you to take a moment, or many, and think about what this means.

I have been doing so, many times. One reason is, because the way Eva emphazised on saying these words – WOW! - this was spectacular!! Her level of focus and concentration and ability to say these words, was actually one of the most remarkable moments of my life. And it goes so deep, what it means! As you probably know, modern stars, kings, pharaos, holy persons throughout the history of mankind have been gracing themselves with jewellery! Yet, the question is, is one rich and wealthy with a huge amount of money and then buys gemstones to showcase this richness? Or is it that one buys gemstones and treasures these artefacts and gets to automatically amass money and wealth because of the presence of these gemstones?

To be honest, I came to understand that both can be true.

One can do phenomenally well and like to grace him-/herself with precious stones in order to display their fortune. Yet I also think that these gemstones have a special frequency and attract more of what they vibrate at. Like attracts alike. Let us dive into detail, what I exactly mean by that:

Quantum physics suggest that everything is energy. We all are vibrating particles and the frequency of these vibrations reflect the frequency of certain characteristics. This applies to us, humans, this applies to any form of matter and therfore does it to gemstones. Gemstones oscillate at a certain frequency. Computer tomographs show that when we as humans feel different states and emotions, we vibrate on respectivly suiting, different frequencies. There is this great matching quote by Dr. Wayne Dyer:

"Abundance is nothing we acquire, Abundance is something we tune into."

When we tune into the frequency of Abundance, our life matches this frequency. As stated before, when we think rich thoughts, life confirms these thoughts in the following with rich experiences. We see and attract more of what we focus our attention on. Therefore the question is, how do we ensure that our thoughts are and stay of rich character?

There are actually many ways, for example the listening to binaural beats, the chanting of certain mantras, affirmations, ..., and the presence of specific gemstones. Gemstones oscillate at a certain frequency, a frequency which is associated with specific qualities, such as Abundance.

I have been fascinated by gemstones for a while and appreciate the effects of every kind I got. There are gemstones enhancing the feeling of confidence, self-worth and certainty about our own right to exist. There are gemstones to support in the attraction of love, pleasure and delight. And there are gemstones, which support the attraction of wealth, prosperity and abundance.

To be completely honest with you, I knew the information of this book, which I have been gathering throughout my life. Yet everything fell into place, in terms of prosperity and wealth, with the sudden presence of my ring, ornamentally adorned with Peridot.

I gifted myself this present on December 24th 2019. Peridot represents the divine love and vibrates this love abundantly on all levels of life. Which makes it a very universal stone to enrich our life with loving relationships, financial plethora and cheerful lightheartedness. Practically speaking, in the following days and weeks after its arrival in my life, I super productively and enthusiastically finished income generating projects, which I started months earlier and somehow did not finish. I wrote and published a myriad of books with ideas over ideas, which just came to me out of the blue and I felt driven to execute them. These books turned into huge successes, especially the one you are reading right now. I automatically felt drawn to inform myself about different assets and acquired very prosperous stocks and shares. I invested in further online education, which made me realise more clearly, what I genuienly love to do more of, in order to progress effectively with my personal legacy. I have always been well on track with my purpose, yet it feels enhanced with the presence of this present.

Other people communicated automatically more appreciation and love for me. These are all the effects of the presence of the Peridot in my life. I am truly fascinated by this and in awe. I believe that the presence of the Peridot tunes my personal frequency on a very subtle and mostly uncoscious level into abundance. From this subconscious and underlying area, thoughts, feelings and actions arise already as the effect. The presence of the Peridot is therefore a root-cause, attuning my being into Prosperity with allowing properous thoughts and actions to happen in the following, which then manifest in physical results, like success in my projects, greater reward in my business endeavours and all other areas, as Peridot brings Abundance in all areas of life. It truly is a very complete and universal gemstone. The energetic potential of a gemstone is not necessarily matched by the price. Yes, diamonds for example are more expensive and I do have a small diamond earstud as well. Yet the effect of the presence of the diamond has not been as outstanding as the one of the Peridot. This is my personal experience, might differ from person to person, yet the truth that gemstones have an effect is universal and real.

Now, I have to raise your awareness about a very special point.

Gemstones are very precious and rare. I believe that it is okay to have a tiny, little bit of the ones we feel most directed to. Still, a hoarding of these precious materials is not what they are intended for and this probably turns into opposite effects. Because where are they coming from? Out of mother earth. Planet earth is such a beautiful, vivid and colourful planet to live on, because of its richness in natural ressources. When we mine all these resources out of mother earth, we leave her not in a good shape. Therefore the individual grace with the precious gifts of mother earth have to transpire in a respectful and conscious manner. I am sure you are also caring about the home you are part of and living on, right?

How to be free now.

To be free, is to be alive and in harmony with the principles of life.

Freedom, full enlightenment, is granted to the ones who live as an apotheosis of life. Which means to think as the perfect embodiment of god in human form. It means to honor and sincerely apply the principles of life. It especially means to live in peaceful, compassionate togetherness with all living beings. Which means, in year 2020, to choose a loving diet and let the feeling animals alive.

To be free, is to be open and curious about the new evolutions of life. To adjust to new endeavours and to choose love, in every moment of now. It is to forgive and love again.

The feeling of true freedom arises over time with having the highest moral standards and applying them as best as possible, always. The progression into the light is automatic and guaranteed. Do good, generously and good streams back to you, generously.

As it goes around, it comes around.

As above, so below.
In the big, in the small.

God and Life sees everything and reacts always accordingly.

Do purely good, generously.

And be free.

May all beings be happy, rich and free!

Sincerely,

Sascha Të Light

BONUS: The way I do business

Because I am doing so well financially and in the way I invest money, others are automatically coming to me and ask me to invest their money for them. After I explain what I do and how I do it, I also explain "how to be paid". My view is this:

I think, people who are really rich, do not rely on other people giving them money. Rich people simply have more than enough any way. I do what I do, also for others, because I am extremely interested in it and am simply happy to share my interest, so others can benefit from it as well. I also know that the more good I am doing for other people, I get it back any way. Every action translates to a certain karmic connotation and life happens according to the karmic balance of each person. The more good I do, especially for others in a generous way, the "better" my karmic balance. Therefore, life is going to grant me with even "better" circumstances. I do not have to receive any payment from the actual person I am investing the money from. I know that life is "paying" me any way, in the form of that person or another person.

In case I have multiplied the initial investment of that person, I am open for that person to give me something for doing so. I completely entrust that person to choose the amount for the favour, with me being absolutely fine in case it is 0.

Do I have to mention that this way of doing business is very, very good?

If yes, it is. ;)

Diclaimer of Liability

Sascha Të Light
Heinrich-Heine-Strasse 22
08491 Limbach/Germany

Best Contact: **saschatelight@mail.com**

ISBN-13: 978-1656907417

Also published by Freiheit. JETZT!:
(Freedom.NOW!)

Sascha Të Light & Nino Anders

Wayne Dyer, Elon Musk, Dalai Lama, Albert Einstein, Bruce Lee, Buddha, Khalil Gibran, Nikola Tesla, Robert Kiyosaki, Dolores Cannon, Jesus Christ, Justin Bieber and more share their wisdom:
Pearls of the Genius

Paperback: 8.99 Euro
Kindle eBook: 124.99 Euro

This book is a dynamic collection of ideas, which are enriching your life comprehensively. Imagine, you could bring your life easy and precise with the greatest ideas of the greatest minds of human history to fruition. Which circumstances become possible?

Live your life in copiousness Now! thanks to your reading of this book.

"Nothing is as strong as an idea whose time has come."

Amazon page: https://amzn.to/3nByJTU

(Also available in German: 'Perlen der Genies'; and Spanish: 'Perlas de Genios')

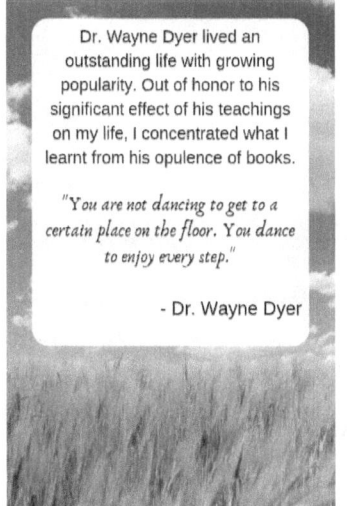

Nino Anders

Heaven on Earth is not a place – It is a Feeling

Paperback: 8.99 Euro

Kindle eBook: 3.29 Euro

(Also available in German: Himmel auf Erden ist kein Ort – Es ist eine Entscheidung.)

Dr. Wayne Dyer was an extraordinary person. With his teachings he inspired & enriched the lives of millions of people.

Choose to live heaven on earth by applying his 55+ highest ideas of wisdom to your life + PLUS the 3 moving farewell speeches of his daughters Saje, Skye and Serena, illustrating how Wayne lived his teachings in everyday life.

Amazon page:

https://amzn.to/2Ld6evH

Joe Dirtay

BITCOIN – The Internet's Money

Why this cryptocurrency is the new Money & how the blockchain came to be for our prosperity

Paperback: 8.99 Euro

Kindle eBook: 3.29 Euro

Gold has been the hardest value preserving asset in history, until now. The inception of BITCOIN marks a new era in finance, with unprecedented opportunities. In this book you are about to read how BITCOIN is structured in such a brilliant way that will revolutionize the way business is done.

Amazon page:

https://amzn.to/2Zsmkrj

In eternal gratitude for your feedback/your opinion/your review:

https://www.amazon.com/dp/B083JPNYTS

www.ingramcontent.com/pod-product-compliance
Lightning Source LLC
Chambersburg PA
CBHW021509210526
45463CB00002B/959